I0788484

FREEDOM TO
SUCCEED

LIFE & BUSINESS PLANNER

THE PROPRIETOR

Name	
Address	
Phone	
Email	

THE BUSINESS

Name	
Legal Status	
Address	
Phone	
Email	
Website	
Strapline	
Facebook	
Instagram	
Twitter	
YouTube	

Trust in the Lord with all thine heart;
and lean not unto thine own understanding.
In all thy ways acknowledge Him,
and He shall direct thy paths.
(PROVERBS 3:5-6)

MONTH: YEAR:

Task	Completed?

MONTHLY TO DO LIST

Task	Completed?

Freedom To Succeed

	MORNING	AFTERNOON	EVENING
1ST			
2ND			
3RD			
4TH			
5TH			
6TH			
7TH			
8TH			
9TH			
10TH			
11TH			
12TH			
13TH			
14TH			
15TH			
16TH			
17TH			
18TH			
19TH			
20TH			
21ST			
22ND			
23RD			
24TH			
25TH			
26TH			
27TH			
28TH			
29TH			
30TH			
31ST			

DATE GOALS SET:

LIFESTYLE (E.G. SLEEP, NUTRITION, PUNCTUALITY ETC.)

FAMILY / SOCIAL

PHYSICAL FITNESS / HEALTH

MENTAL / EMOTIONAL / SPIRITUAL

WORK / EDUCATION

REVIEW YOUR GOALS AT THE END OF THE MONTH.
DID YOU ACHIEVE THEM? IF YES, WHAT WORKED WELL?
IF NOT, WHAT WILL YOU DO DIFFERENTLY NEXT MONTH?

LIFESTYLE (E.G. SLEEP, NUTRITION, PUNCTUALITY ETC.)

FAMILY / SOCIAL

PHYSICAL FITNESS / HEALTH

MENTAL / EMOTIONAL / SPIRITUAL

WORK / EDUCATION

DATE OF REVIEW:

WEEK STARTING:

MONDAY

TUESDAY

WEDNESDAY

THURSDAY

FRIDAY

SATURDAY

SUNDAY

NOTES

WEEK STARTING:

MONDAY

TUESDAY

WEDNESDAY

THURSDAY

FRIDAY

SATURDAY

SUNDAY

NOTES

WEEK STARTING:

MONDAY

TUESDAY

WEDNESDAY

THURSDAY

FRIDAY

SATURDAY

SUNDAY

NOTES

WEEK STARTING:

MONDAY

TUESDAY

WEDNESDAY

THURSDAY

FRIDAY

SATURDAY

SUNDAY

NOTES

WEEK STARTING:

MONDAY

TUESDAY

WEDNESDAY

THURSDAY

FRIDAY

SATURDAY

SUNDAY

NOTES

The thoughts of the diligent tend only to plenteousness;
but of every one that is hasty only to want.
(PROVERBS 21:5)

MONTH: YEAR:

Task	Completed?

Task	Completed?

Freedom To Succeed

	MORNING	AFTERNOON	EVENING
1ST			
2ND			
3RD			
4TH			
5TH			
6TH			
7TH			
8TH			
9TH			
10TH			
11TH			
12TH			
13TH			
14TH			
15TH			
16TH			
17TH			
18TH			
19TH			
20TH			
21ST			
22ND			
23RD			
24TH			
25TH			
26TH			
27TH			
28TH			
29TH			
30TH			
31ST			

DATE GOALS SET:

LIFESTYLE (E.G. SLEEP, NUTRITION, PUNCTUALITY ETC.)

FAMILY / SOCIAL

PHYSICAL FITNESS / HEALTH

MENTAL / EMOTIONAL / SPIRITUAL

WORK / EDUCATION

REVIEW YOUR GOALS AT THE END OF THE MONTH.
DID YOU ACHIEVE THEM? IF YES, WHAT WORKED WELL?
IF NOT, WHAT WILL YOU DO DIFFERENTLY NEXT MONTH?

LIFESTYLE (E.G. SLEEP, NUTRITION, PUNCTUALITY ETC.)

FAMILY / SOCIAL

PHYSICAL FITNESS / HEALTH

MENTAL / EMOTIONAL / SPIRITUAL

WORK / EDUCATION

DATE OF REVIEW:

WEEK STARTING:

MONDAY

TUESDAY

WEDNESDAY

THURSDAY

FRIDAY

SATURDAY

SUNDAY

NOTES

WEEK STARTING:

MONDAY

TUESDAY

WEDNESDAY

THURSDAY

FRIDAY

SATURDAY

SUNDAY

NOTES

WEEK STARTING:

MONDAY

TUESDAY

WEDNESDAY

THURSDAY

FRIDAY

SATURDAY

SUNDAY

NOTES

WEEK STARTING:

MONDAY

TUESDAY

WEDNESDAY

THURSDAY

FRIDAY

SATURDAY

SUNDAY

NOTES

WEEK STARTING:

MONDAY

TUESDAY

WEDNESDAY

THURSDAY

FRIDAY

SATURDAY

SUNDAY

NOTES

And whatsoever ye do, do it heartily,
as to the Lord, and not unto men;
(COLOSSIANS 3:23)

MONTH: YEAR:

Task	Completed?

Task	Completed?

	MORNING	AFTERNOON	EVENING
1ST			
2ND			
3RD			
4TH			
5TH			
6TH			
7TH			
8TH			
9TH			
10TH			
11TH			
12TH			
13TH			
14TH			
15TH			
16TH			
17TH			
18TH			
19TH			
20TH			
21ST			
22ND			
23RD			
24TH			
25TH			
26TH			
27TH			
28TH			
29TH			
30TH			
31ST			

DATE GOALS SET:

LIFESTYLE (E.G. SLEEP, NUTRITION, PUNCTUALITY ETC.)

FAMILY / SOCIAL

PHYSICAL FITNESS / HEALTH

MENTAL / EMOTIONAL / SPIRITUAL

WORK / EDUCATION

REVIEW YOUR GOALS AT THE END OF THE MONTH.
DID YOU ACHIEVE THEM? IF YES, WHAT WORKED WELL?
IF NOT, WHAT WILL YOU DO DIFFERENTLY NEXT MONTH?

LIFESTYLE (E.G. SLEEP, NUTRITION, PUNCTUALITY ETC.)

FAMILY / SOCIAL

PHYSICAL FITNESS / HEALTH

MENTAL / EMOTIONAL / SPIRITUAL

WORK / EDUCATION

DATE OF REVIEW:

WEEK STARTING:

MONDAY

TUESDAY

WEDNESDAY

THURSDAY

FRIDAY

SATURDAY

SUNDAY

NOTES

WEEK STARTING:

MONDAY

TUESDAY

WEDNESDAY

THURSDAY

FRIDAY

SATURDAY

SUNDAY

NOTES

WEEK STARTING:

MONDAY

TUESDAY

WEDNESDAY

THURSDAY

FRIDAY

SATURDAY

SUNDAY

NOTES

WEEK STARTING:

MONDAY

TUESDAY

WEDNESDAY

THURSDAY

FRIDAY

SATURDAY

SUNDAY

NOTES

WEEK STARTING:

MONDAY

TUESDAY

WEDNESDAY

THURSDAY

FRIDAY

SATURDAY

SUNDAY

NOTES

In all labour there is profit:
but the talk of the lips tendeth only to penury.
(PROVERBS 14:23)

MONTH: YEAR:

Task	Completed?

Task	Completed?

	MORNING	AFTERNOON	EVENING
1ST			
2ND			
3RD			
4TH			
5TH			
6TH			
7TH			
8TH			
9TH			
10TH			
11TH			
12TH			
13TH			
14TH			
15TH			
16TH			
17TH			
18TH			
19TH			
20TH			
21ST			
22ND			
23RD			
24TH			
25TH			
26TH			
27TH			
28TH			
29TH			
30TH			
31ST			

DATE GOALS SET:

LIFESTYLE (E.G. SLEEP, NUTRITION, PUNCTUALITY ETC.)

FAMILY / SOCIAL

PHYSICAL FITNESS / HEALTH

MENTAL / EMOTIONAL / SPIRITUAL

WORK / EDUCATION

REVIEW YOUR GOALS AT THE END OF THE MONTH.
DID YOU ACHIEVE THEM? IF YES, WHAT WORKED WELL?
IF NOT, WHAT WILL YOU DO DIFFERENTLY NEXT MONTH?

LIFESTYLE (E.G. SLEEP, NUTRITION, PUNCTUALITY ETC.)

FAMILY / SOCIAL

PHYSICAL FITNESS / HEALTH

MENTAL / EMOTIONAL / SPIRITUAL

WORK / EDUCATION

DATE OF REVIEW:

WEEK STARTING:

MONDAY

TUESDAY

WEDNESDAY

THURSDAY

FRIDAY

SATURDAY

SUNDAY

NOTES

WEEK STARTING:

MONDAY

TUESDAY

WEDNESDAY

THURSDAY

FRIDAY

SATURDAY

SUNDAY

NOTES

WEEK STARTING:

MONDAY

TUESDAY

WEDNESDAY

THURSDAY

FRIDAY

SATURDAY

SUNDAY

NOTES

WEEK STARTING:

MONDAY

TUESDAY

WEDNESDAY

THURSDAY

FRIDAY

SATURDAY

SUNDAY

NOTES

WEEK STARTING:

MONDAY

TUESDAY

WEDNESDAY

THURSDAY

FRIDAY

SATURDAY

SUNDAY

NOTES

In the morning sow thy seed,
and in the evening withhold not thine hand:
for thou knowest not whether shall prosper,
either this or that,
or whether they both shall be alike good.
(ECCLESIASTES 11:6)

MONTH: YEAR:

Task	Completed?

Task	Completed?

	MORNING	AFTERNOON	EVENING
1ST			
2ND			
3RD			
4TH			
5TH			
6TH			
7TH			
8TH			
9TH			
10TH			
11TH			
12TH			
13TH			
14TH			
15TH			
16TH			
17TH			
18TH			
19TH			
20TH			
21ST			
22ND			
23RD			
24TH			
25TH			
26TH			
27TH			
28TH			
29TH			
30TH			
31ST			

DATE GOALS SET:

LIFESTYLE (E.G. SLEEP, NUTRITION, PUNCTUALITY ETC.)

FAMILY / SOCIAL

PHYSICAL FITNESS / HEALTH

MENTAL / EMOTIONAL / SPIRITUAL

WORK / EDUCATION

REVIEW YOUR GOALS AT THE END OF THE MONTH.
DID YOU ACHIEVE THEM? IF YES, WHAT WORKED WELL?
IF NOT, WHAT WILL YOU DO DIFFERENTLY NEXT MONTH?

LIFESTYLE (E.G. SLEEP, NUTRITION, PUNCTUALITY ETC.)

FAMILY / SOCIAL

PHYSICAL FITNESS / HEALTH

MENTAL / EMOTIONAL / SPIRITUAL

WORK / EDUCATION

DATE OF REVIEW:

WEEK STARTING:

MONDAY

TUESDAY

WEDNESDAY

THURSDAY

FRIDAY

SATURDAY

SUNDAY

NOTES

WEEK STARTING:

MONDAY

TUESDAY

WEDNESDAY

THURSDAY

FRIDAY

SATURDAY

SUNDAY

NOTES

WEEK STARTING:

MONDAY

TUESDAY

WEDNESDAY

THURSDAY

FRIDAY

SATURDAY

SUNDAY

NOTES

WEEK STARTING:

MONDAY

TUESDAY

WEDNESDAY

THURSDAY

FRIDAY

SATURDAY

SUNDAY

NOTES

WEEK STARTING:

MONDAY

TUESDAY

WEDNESDAY

THURSDAY

FRIDAY

SATURDAY

SUNDAY

NOTES

Commit thy works unto the Lord,
and thy thoughts shall be established.
(PROVERBS 16:3)

MONTH: YEAR:

Task   *Completed?*

Task	Completed?

	MORNING	AFTERNOON	EVENING
1ST			
2ND			
3RD			
4TH			
5TH			
6TH			
7TH			
8TH			
9TH			
10TH			
11TH			
12TH			
13TH			
14TH			
15TH			
16TH			
17TH			
18TH			
19TH			
20TH			
21ST			
22ND			
23RD			
24TH			
25TH			
26TH			
27TH			
28TH			
29TH			
30TH			
31ST			

DATE GOALS SET:

LIFESTYLE (E.G. SLEEP, NUTRITION, PUNCTUALITY ETC.)

FAMILY / SOCIAL

PHYSICAL FITNESS / HEALTH

MENTAL / EMOTIONAL / SPIRITUAL

WORK / EDUCATION

REVIEW YOUR GOALS AT THE END OF THE MONTH.
DID YOU ACHIEVE THEM? IF YES, WHAT WORKED WELL?
IF NOT, WHAT WILL YOU DO DIFFERENTLY NEXT MONTH?

LIFESTYLE (E.G. SLEEP, NUTRITION, PUNCTUALITY ETC.)

FAMILY / SOCIAL

PHYSICAL FITNESS / HEALTH

MENTAL / EMOTIONAL / SPIRITUAL

WORK / EDUCATION

DATE OF REVIEW:

WEEK STARTING:

MONDAY

TUESDAY

WEDNESDAY

THURSDAY

FRIDAY

SATURDAY

SUNDAY

NOTES

WEEK STARTING:

MONDAY

TUESDAY

WEDNESDAY

THURSDAY

FRIDAY

SATURDAY

SUNDAY

NOTES

WEEK STARTING:

MONDAY

TUESDAY

WEDNESDAY

THURSDAY

FRIDAY

SATURDAY

SUNDAY

NOTES

WEEK STARTING:

MONDAY

TUESDAY

WEDNESDAY

THURSDAY

FRIDAY

SATURDAY

SUNDAY

NOTES

WEEK STARTING:

MONDAY

TUESDAY

WEDNESDAY

THURSDAY

FRIDAY

SATURDAY

SUNDAY

NOTES

But thou shalt remember the Lord thy God:
for it is He that giveth thee power to get wealth,
that He may establish His covenant which He sware unto
thy fathers, as it is this day.
(DEUTERONOMY 8:18)

MONTH: YEAR:

Task	Completed?

MONTHLY TO DO LIST

Task	Completed?

MONTHLY SCHEDULE

	MORNING	AFTERNOON	EVENING
1ST			
2ND			
3RD			
4TH			
5TH			
6TH			
7TH			
8TH			
9TH			
10TH			
11TH			
12TH			
13TH			
14TH			
15TH			
16TH			
17TH			
18TH			
19TH			
20TH			
21ST			
22ND			
23RD			
24TH			
25TH			
26TH			
27TH			
28TH			
29TH			
30TH			
31ST			

DATE GOALS SET:

LIFESTYLE (E.G. SLEEP, NUTRITION, PUNCTUALITY ETC.)

FAMILY / SOCIAL

PHYSICAL FITNESS / HEALTH

MENTAL / EMOTIONAL / SPIRITUAL

WORK / EDUCATION

REVIEW YOUR GOALS AT THE END OF THE MONTH.
DID YOU ACHIEVE THEM? IF YES, WHAT WORKED WELL?
IF NOT, WHAT WILL YOU DO DIFFERENTLY NEXT MONTH?

LIFESTYLE (E.G. SLEEP, NUTRITION, PUNCTUALITY ETC.)

FAMILY / SOCIAL

PHYSICAL FITNESS / HEALTH

MENTAL / EMOTIONAL / SPIRITUAL

WORK / EDUCATION

DATE OF REVIEW:

WEEK STARTING:

MONDAY

TUESDAY

WEDNESDAY

THURSDAY

FRIDAY

SATURDAY

SUNDAY

NOTES

WEEK STARTING:

MONDAY

TUESDAY

WEDNESDAY

THURSDAY

FRIDAY

SATURDAY

SUNDAY

NOTES

WEEK STARTING:

MONDAY

TUESDAY

WEDNESDAY

THURSDAY

FRIDAY

SATURDAY

SUNDAY

NOTES

WEEK STARTING:

<table>
<tr><td>MONDAY

</td></tr>
<tr><td>TUESDAY

</td></tr>
<tr><td>WEDNESDAY

</td></tr>
<tr><td>THURSDAY

</td></tr>
</table>

FRIDAY

SATURDAY

SUNDAY

NOTES

WEEK STARTING:

MONDAY

TUESDAY

WEDNESDAY

THURSDAY

FRIDAY

SATURDAY

SUNDAY

NOTES

I can do all things through Christ which strengtheneth me.
(PHILIPPIANS 4:13)

MONTH: **YEAR:**

Task	Completed?

Task	Completed?

	MORNING	AFTERNOON	EVENING
1ST			
2ND			
3RD			
4TH			
5TH			
6TH			
7TH			
8TH			
9TH			
10TH			
11TH			
12TH			
13TH			
14TH			
15TH			
16TH			
17TH			
18TH			
19TH			
20TH			
21ST			
22ND			
23RD			
24TH			
25TH			
26TH			
27TH			
28TH			
29TH			
30TH			
31ST			

DATE GOALS SET:

LIFESTYLE (E.G. SLEEP, NUTRITION, PUNCTUALITY ETC.)
FAMILY / SOCIAL
PHYSICAL FITNESS / HEALTH
MENTAL / EMOTIONAL / SPIRITUAL
WORK / EDUCATION

REVIEW YOUR GOALS AT THE END OF THE MONTH.
DID YOU ACHIEVE THEM? IF YES, WHAT WORKED WELL?
IF NOT, WHAT WILL YOU DO DIFFERENTLY NEXT MONTH?

LIFESTYLE (E.G. SLEEP, NUTRITION, PUNCTUALITY ETC.)

FAMILY / SOCIAL

PHYSICAL FITNESS / HEALTH

MENTAL / EMOTIONAL / SPIRITUAL

WORK / EDUCATION

DATE OF REVIEW:

WEEK STARTING:

MONDAY

TUESDAY

WEDNESDAY

THURSDAY

FRIDAY

SATURDAY

SUNDAY

NOTES

WEEK STARTING:

MONDAY

TUESDAY

WEDNESDAY

THURSDAY

FRIDAY

SATURDAY

SUNDAY

NOTES

WEEK STARTING:

MONDAY

TUESDAY

WEDNESDAY

THURSDAY

FRIDAY

SATURDAY

SUNDAY

NOTES

WEEK STARTING:

MONDAY

TUESDAY

WEDNESDAY

THURSDAY

Freedom To Succeed

FRIDAY

SATURDAY

SUNDAY

NOTES

WEEK STARTING:

MONDAY

TUESDAY

WEDNESDAY

THURSDAY

FRIDAY

SATURDAY

SUNDAY

NOTES

And the Lord answered me, and said,
Write the vision, and make it plain upon tables,
that he may run that readeth it.
(HABAKKUK 2:2)

MONTH: YEAR:

Task	Completed?

Task	Completed?

	MORNING	AFTERNOON	EVENING
1ST			
2ND			
3RD			
4TH			
5TH			
6TH			
7TH			
8TH			
9TH			
10TH			
11TH			
12TH			
13TH			
14TH			
15TH			
16TH			
17TH			
18TH			
19TH			
20TH			
21ST			
22ND			
23RD			
24TH			
25TH			
26TH			
27TH			
28TH			
29TH			
30TH			
31ST			

DATE GOALS SET:

LIFESTYLE (E.G. SLEEP, NUTRITION, PUNCTUALITY ETC.)

FAMILY / SOCIAL

PHYSICAL FITNESS / HEALTH

MENTAL / EMOTIONAL / SPIRITUAL

WORK / EDUCATION

REVIEW YOUR GOALS AT THE END OF THE MONTH.
DID YOU ACHIEVE THEM? IF YES, WHAT WORKED WELL?
IF NOT, WHAT WILL YOU DO DIFFERENTLY NEXT MONTH?

LIFESTYLE (E.G. SLEEP, NUTRITION, PUNCTUALITY ETC.)

FAMILY / SOCIAL

PHYSICAL FITNESS / HEALTH

MENTAL / EMOTIONAL / SPIRITUAL

WORK / EDUCATION

DATE OF REVIEW:

WEEK STARTING:

MONDAY

TUESDAY

WEDNESDAY

THURSDAY

FRIDAY

SATURDAY

SUNDAY

NOTES

WEEK STARTING:

MONDAY

TUESDAY

WEDNESDAY

THURSDAY

FRIDAY

SATURDAY

SUNDAY

NOTES

WEEK STARTING:

MONDAY

TUESDAY

WEDNESDAY

THURSDAY

FRIDAY

SATURDAY

SUNDAY

NOTES

WEEK STARTING:

MONDAY

TUESDAY

WEDNESDAY

THURSDAY

FRIDAY

SATURDAY

SUNDAY

NOTES

WEEK STARTING:

MONDAY

TUESDAY

WEDNESDAY

THURSDAY

FRIDAY

SATURDAY

SUNDAY

NOTES

And be not conformed to this world:
but be ye transformed by the renewing of your mind,
that ye may prove what is that good, and acceptable,
and perfect, will of God.
(ROMANS 12:2)

MONTH: YEAR:

Task	Completed?

Task	Completed?

	MORNING	AFTERNOON	EVENING
1ST			
2ND			
3RD			
4TH			
5TH			
6TH			
7TH			
8TH			
9TH			
10TH			
11TH			
12TH			
13TH			
14TH			
15TH			
16TH			
17TH			
18TH			
19TH			
20TH			
21ST			
22ND			
23RD			
24TH			
25TH			
26TH			
27TH			
28TH			
29TH			
30TH			
31ST			

DATE GOALS SET:

LIFESTYLE (E.G. SLEEP, NUTRITION, PUNCTUALITY ETC.)

FAMILY / SOCIAL

PHYSICAL FITNESS / HEALTH

MENTAL / EMOTIONAL / SPIRITUAL

WORK / EDUCATION

REVIEW YOUR GOALS AT THE END OF THE MONTH.
DID YOU ACHIEVE THEM? IF YES, WHAT WORKED WELL?
IF NOT, WHAT WILL YOU DO DIFFERENTLY NEXT MONTH?

LIFESTYLE (E.G. SLEEP, NUTRITION, PUNCTUALITY ETC.)

FAMILY / SOCIAL

PHYSICAL FITNESS / HEALTH

MENTAL / EMOTIONAL / SPIRITUAL

WORK / EDUCATION

DATE OF REVIEW:

WEEK STARTING:

MONDAY

TUESDAY

WEDNESDAY

THURSDAY

FRIDAY

SATURDAY

SUNDAY

NOTES

WEEK STARTING:

MONDAY

TUESDAY

WEDNESDAY

THURSDAY

FRIDAY

SATURDAY

SUNDAY

NOTES

WEEK STARTING:

MONDAY

TUESDAY

WEDNESDAY

THURSDAY

FRIDAY

SATURDAY

SUNDAY

NOTES

WEEK STARTING:

MONDAY

TUESDAY

WEDNESDAY

THURSDAY

FRIDAY

SATURDAY

SUNDAY

NOTES

WEEK STARTING:

MONDAY

TUESDAY

WEDNESDAY

THURSDAY

FRIDAY

SATURDAY

SUNDAY

NOTES

A man's gift maketh room for him,
and bringeth him before great men.
(PROVERBS 18:16)

MONTH: YEAR:

Task	Completed?

Task	Completed?

	MORNING	AFTERNOON	EVENING
1ST			
2ND			
3RD			
4TH			
5TH			
6TH			
7TH			
8TH			
9TH			
10TH			
11TH			
12TH			
13TH			
14TH			
15TH			
16TH			
17TH			
18TH			
19TH			
20TH			
21ST			
22ND			
23RD			
24TH			
25TH			
26TH			
27TH			
28TH			
29TH			
30TH			
31ST			

DATE GOALS SET:

LIFESTYLE (E.G. SLEEP, NUTRITION, PUNCTUALITY ETC.)

FAMILY / SOCIAL

PHYSICAL FITNESS / HEALTH

MENTAL / EMOTIONAL / SPIRITUAL

WORK / EDUCATION

REVIEW YOUR GOALS AT THE END OF THE MONTH.
DID YOU ACHIEVE THEM? IF YES, WHAT WORKED WELL?
IF NOT, WHAT WILL YOU DO DIFFERENTLY NEXT MONTH?

LIFESTYLE (E.G. SLEEP, NUTRITION, PUNCTUALITY ETC.)

FAMILY / SOCIAL

PHYSICAL FITNESS / HEALTH

MENTAL / EMOTIONAL / SPIRITUAL

WORK / EDUCATION

DATE OF REVIEW:

WEEK STARTING:

MONDAY

TUESDAY

WEDNESDAY

THURSDAY

FRIDAY

SATURDAY

SUNDAY

NOTES

WEEK STARTING:

MONDAY

TUESDAY

WEDNESDAY

THURSDAY

FRIDAY

SATURDAY

SUNDAY

NOTES

WEEK STARTING:

MONDAY

TUESDAY

WEDNESDAY

THURSDAY

FRIDAY

SATURDAY

SUNDAY

NOTES

WEEK STARTING:

MONDAY

TUESDAY

WEDNESDAY

THURSDAY

FRIDAY

SATURDAY

SUNDAY

NOTES

WEEK STARTING:

MONDAY

TUESDAY

WEDNESDAY

THURSDAY

FRIDAY

SATURDAY

SUNDAY

NOTES

MONTH: YEAR:

Task	Completed?

Task	Completed?

	MORNING	AFTERNOON	EVENING
1ST			
2ND			
3RD			
4TH			
5TH			
6TH			
7TH			
8TH			
9TH			
10TH			
11TH			
12TH			
13TH			
14TH			
15TH			
16TH			
17TH			
18TH			
19TH			
20TH			
21ST			
22ND			
23RD			
24TH			
25TH			
26TH			
27TH			
28TH			
29TH			
30TH			
31ST			

DATE GOALS SET:

LIFESTYLE (E.G. SLEEP, NUTRITION, PUNCTUALITY ETC.)

FAMILY / SOCIAL

PHYSICAL FITNESS / HEALTH

MENTAL / EMOTIONAL / SPIRITUAL

WORK / EDUCATION

REVIEW YOUR GOALS AT THE END OF THE MONTH.
DID YOU ACHIEVE THEM? IF YES, WHAT WORKED WELL?
IF NOT, WHAT WILL YOU DO DIFFERENTLY NEXT MONTH?

LIFESTYLE (E.G. SLEEP, NUTRITION, PUNCTUALITY ETC.)

FAMILY / SOCIAL

PHYSICAL FITNESS / HEALTH

MENTAL / EMOTIONAL / SPIRITUAL

WORK / EDUCATION

DATE OF REVIEW:

WEEK STARTING:

MONDAY

TUESDAY

WEDNESDAY

THURSDAY

FRIDAY

SATURDAY

SUNDAY

NOTES

WEEK STARTING:

MONDAY

TUESDAY

WEDNESDAY

THURSDAY

FRIDAY

SATURDAY

SUNDAY

NOTES

WEEK STARTING:

MONDAY

TUESDAY

WEDNESDAY

THURSDAY

FRIDAY

SATURDAY

SUNDAY

NOTES

WEEK STARTING:

MONDAY

TUESDAY

WEDNESDAY

THURSDAY

FRIDAY

SATURDAY

SUNDAY

NOTES

WEEK STARTING:

MONDAY

TUESDAY

WEDNESDAY

THURSDAY

FRIDAY

SATURDAY

SUNDAY

NOTES

NOTES

NOTES

NOTES